THE STORY OF CHRISTMAS

words from the Gospels of Matthew and Luke

THE STORY OF CHRISTMAS

CHRISTMAS

pictures by Jane Ray

DUTTON CHILDREN'S BOOKS   NEW YORK

for Ellen

The words from the Gospels of Matthew and Luke have been taken from the Authorized King James Version of the Bible.

Illustrations copyright © 1991 by Jane Ray

All rights reserved.

CIP Data is available.

First published in the United States 1991 by
Dutton Children's Books,
a division of Penguin Books USA Inc.

Originally published 1991 in Great Britain by
Orchard Books, the Watts Group,
96 Leonard Street, London EC2A 4RH

First American Edition   Printed in Singapore
10 9 8 7 6 5 4 3 2 1
Spanish edition available
ISBN 0-525-44768-7

In the days of Herod, the king of Judea, there was a virgin espoused to a man named Joseph. She lived in the city of Nazareth, and her name was Mary.

And the angel Gabriel was sent from God unto her, and said,
Hail, thou that art highly favored, the Lord is with thee:
blessed art thou among women. Fear not, for thou shalt bring
forth a son, and shalt call his name Jesus. He shall be great,

and shall be called the Son of the Highest; and of his
kingdom there shall be no end. And Mary said, Behold
the handmaid of the Lord; be it unto me according
to thy word. And the angel departed from her.

And it came to pass in those days, that there
went out a decree from Caesar Augustus that

all the world should be taxed. So all went
to be taxed, every one into his own city.

And Joseph also went into Judea, to be taxed

with Mary his espoused wife, being great with child.

And so it was, that, while they were there, in
the city of David, which is called Bethlehem,

And there were in the same country shepherds abiding in the field, keeping watch over their flock by night. And, lo, the angel of the Lord came upon them, and the glory of the Lord shone round about them: and they were sore afraid. And the angel said unto them, Fear not: for, behold, I bring you good

tidings of great joy, which shall be to all people. For unto
you is born this day in the city of David a Savior, which is
Christ the Lord. And this shall be a sign unto you; Ye shall
find the babe wrapped in swaddling clothes, lying in a manger.

And suddenly there was with the angel a multitude
of the heavenly host praising God, and saying,

Glory to God in the highest, and on earth peace,
good will toward men.

As the angels were gone away from them into heaven, the shepherds said to one another, Let us now go even unto Bethlehem, and see this thing which

And when they had seen it, they made known abroad
the saying which was told them concerning this child.

the Lord hath made known unto us. And they
came with haste, and found Mary, and Joseph,
and the babe lying in a manger.

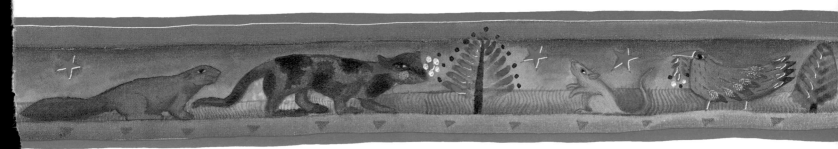

Now when Jesus was born in Bethlehem of Judea in the days
of Herod the king, behold, there came wise men from the east

And all they that heard it wondered at those things which were told them by the shepherds.

to Jerusalem, Saying, Where is he that is born King of the Jews? for we have seen his star in the east, and are come to worship him.

When Herod the king had heard these things, he was troubled, and all Jerusalem with him. Then Herod, when he had privily called the wise men, enquired of them diligently what time the star appeared.

And he sent them to Bethlehem, and said, Go and search
diligently for the young child; and when ye have found him,
bring me word again, that I may come and worship him also.

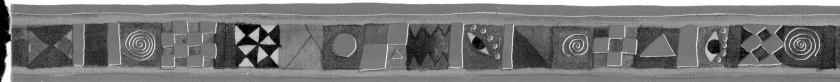

When they had heard the king, they departed;
and, lo, the star, which they saw in the east,

went before them, till it came and stood over
where the young child was.

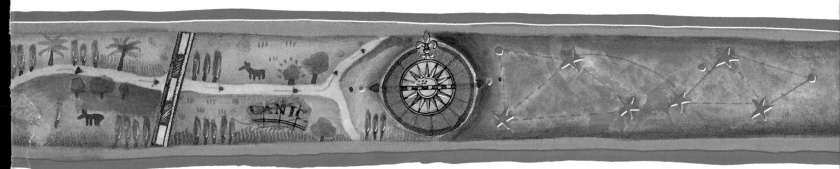

And they saw the young child with Mary his mother, and fell down, and worshipped him and when they had opened their treasures, they presented unto him gifts: gold, and frankincense, and myrrh. And being warned of God that they should not return to Herod, they departed into their own country.

And behold, the angel of the Lord appeareth to Joseph, saying, Arise, and take the young child and his mother, and flee into Egypt; for Herod will seek to destroy him. When he arose, he took the child and his mother, and departed into Egypt.

But when Herod was dead, Joseph took the young child and
his mother, and returned to Nazareth. And the child grew,
and waxed strong in spirit: and the grace of God was upon him.